HYSTERICALLY
HISTORICAL

Hysterically Historical

Gordon Snell

Illustrated by Wendy Shea

Hutchinson

London Sydney Auckland Johannesburg

I give these lines with love, in dedication
To dearest Maeve, who was their inspiration.

First published in 1990 by Hutchinson Children's Books
An imprint of Random Century Group Ltd
20 Vauxhall Bridge Road, London SW1V 2SA

Random Century Australia (Pty) Ltd
20 Alfred Street, Sydney, NSW 2061

Random Century New Zealand Ltd
PO Box 40–086, Glenfield, Auckland 10, New Zealand

Random Century South Africa (Pty) Ltd
PO Box 337, Bergvlei, 2012, South Africa

Printed and bound in Great Britain by
Mackays of Chatham Plc, Chatham, Kent

British Library Cataloguing in Publication Data

Snell, Gordon
Hysterially historical.
I. Title
821.914

ISBN 0-09-176350-9

Contents

Queen Boadicea

In every chariot-driving test
Queen Boadicea was the best;
She drove so well along the road,
She never squashed a single toad.
And yet, whenever there was need,
The Queen could go at breakneck speed;
And when the Grand Prix came along
Her driving skills amazed the throng.

Her challengers just went to bits:
They saw her roar into the pits,
And in one minute change a wheel
While gulping down a three-course meal —
And when she'd won the race, of course
She gave champagne to every horse.

They say Ben Hur, the charioteer,
Once made a guest appearance here.
Five days they raced, the Queen and Ben,
To John O'Groats and back again.
The Umpire said: 'My loyal heart stirs —
The victory is *hers*, not Hur's!'

One day, her High Priest told the Queen,
'Look how improved our roads have been.
I think that I can read the omens:
We're being invaded by the Romans!'

Queen Boadicea drew her sword.
'We'll kick those Romans out!' she roared.
'We'll mince them up into spaghetti
And scatter them like pink confetti!'

For months she drove about the land
Leading her gallant warrior band,
And oh, what fear her foes did feel
To hear her thundering chariot-wheel,
While many a Legionnaire from Rome
Began to wish he'd stayed at home.

No braver chief was ever seen
Than Boadicea, Warrior Queen!

King Arthur and His Knights

King Arthur said: 'I've always found
It's best to make the Table round;
That way, the Knights can't bawl and bleat
If someone's got a better seat.
It's good, too, for the poker school —
Though not much use for shooting Pool!'

One night, when they were feasting there
On moose, and goose, and grizzly bear,
The King said: 'Lads! We need a Quest —
It's time I put you to the test.

'There must be Dragons to be slain,
And realms where wicked Ogres reign,
And Damsels in Distress to save —
And lots of ways to prove you're brave!'

One grumpy Knight growled: 'Can't it wait?'
That armour's what I really hate.
It's just like dressing in a kettle —
And I'm not into Heavy Metal!'

The King said: 'Very well then, stay —
I'll tell my story of the day
I met the Lady of the Lake;
And this time, try to keep awake!'

The Knights fled in a wild stampede:
They'd rather hazard any deed
Than stay and once again be bored
By Arthur's story of his Sword.

They each went off upon a quest,
But Lancelot knew that *his* was best:
With many a courtly wink and leer,
He sought the love of Guinevere —
Which really wasn't very loyal,
For after all, she *was* a Royal!

The problem with such Palace capers
Is trying to keep them from the papers —
And soon each cuddle and caress
Was featured in the tabloid press,
Which really made things very hot
For Guinevere and Lancelot —
Although it earned a handsome salary
For social scribes like Thomas Malory.

King Alfred the Great

King Alfred sat, and racked his brains:
How could he dish those dreadful Danes?
The place was overrun by men
With names like Guthrum, Lars, and Sven.

He thought: 'I'll imitate the spies,
And don a devious disguise.'
So, pocketing his tell-tale crown,
He left a note: 'I'm out of town.'

When nightfall came, he chanced to see
A friendly local B. and B.
The lady said: 'I've done some baking,
So will you watch these cakes I'm making?'

She went away, and soon returned
To find the cakes completely burned;
For Kings do very little cooking,
And Alfred simply wasn't looking.

So then he dressed in harper's gear;
The Danes declared: 'You're welcome here —
Come in and entertain us, do!
And have some Danish lager too.'

Then when they slept, the King began
To copy out their battle plan.
And that is how King Alfred scored
Against the blond, invading horde.

His treaty said, if plunder ceased,
The Danes could have the North and East;
Which went down well in Wessex, yes —
But didn't wow them in Skegness.

Yet Alfred earned the title Great:
He did his best to educate,
To build a navy for the nation,
And give us Latin in translation.

In view of all that he achieved,
King Alfred surely would have grieved
To know that all it really takes
To gain great fame, is burning cakes.

King Canute

The courtiers of King Canute
Would queue to lick his royal boot;
They fawned and flattered, cringed and bowed —
In fact, they were a sickening crowd!

They said: 'We hail the great Canute,
Whose royal power is absolute:
Even the Sea will do his bidding.'
To which the King replied: 'You're kidding!'
'No, no!' the servile courtiers cried,
'Canute can even stop the tide.'

The King said: 'Right! I want you each
To come with me to Brighton Beach.'
The courtiers cheered: 'Hip, hip, hooray!
We'd love a seaside holiday,
With chunks of candy floss to lick,
And funny hats saying: "Kiss Me Quick!".'

The deck-chair man said: 'Royal Sire,
I've got some lovely chairs for hire.'
The King took out his folding throne
And said: 'No, thanks — I've brought my own.'

He sat there on his royal seat
Till waves came lapping at his feet,
And then he cried: 'Now, slobbering slaves,
I'll show you just who rules the waves.
It's not Britannia, you'll agree —
In fact, it isn't even *me*!
I shout: "Go Back! Go Back!" — and yet
You see, I'm getting very wet.'

The frightened courtiers looked at him,
Remembering that they couldn't swim!
The sea engulfed that servile crew,
But King Canute was far from blue:
That wily King had always known
The value of a floating throne!

He stepped out safely on the shore
And said: 'A wise King knows the score.
To rule the waves he does not try —
That way, his royal toes stay dry!'

Macbeth

Three Witches stirred their ghastly brew,
And said: 'Macbeth, we've news for *you*!
To gain a crown you've every hope —
It's written in your horoscope.'

Macbeth went home and told his wife;
She rather fancied Palace life,
And so, when Duncan came to stay,
He didn't see the light of day.

His sons said: 'It was not polite
To make us orphans, overnight.
If this is Scottish hospitality,
We're moving to a new locality!'

Still feeling insecure, Macbeth
Had noble Banquo put to death —
But looking pale and somewhat thinner,
He turned up for the Burns Night Dinner.

Back on the heath, Macbeth was shown
Visions that chilled him to the bone.
Meanwhile, his poor sleepwalking Queen
Just couldn't get her fingers clean.

When many armies came to get him,
Macbeth said nothing could upset him
Unless a Walking Wood appeared —
And then he saw just what he feared!

It wasn't long before Macduff
Had come along and done his stuff.
He showed the rest the tyrant's head
To prove that he was good and dead.

So, though you long for power and riches,
Remember: steer well clear of Witches!

Lady Godiva

Godiva was a kindly girl,
Unlike her spouse, the wicked Earl.
He taxed his people to the hilt —
Non-payment meant that blood was spilt:
Each luckless debtor lost his life,
Which much distressed the Earl's fair wife.

She pleaded: 'If you'll show some pity,
I'll ride quite naked through the city.'
He never thought she'd really dare —
But there she was next morning, bare!
The grooms their joy could hardly stifle,
For truly, she was quite an eyefull.

When she set out upon her ride,
The citizens all stayed inside.
With shutters closed, their eyes they hid —
At least, that's what they *said* they did!

But Peeping Tom, the silly dope,
Went off and fetched his telescope.
He said: 'I'd love to peep at *her*!' —
And thus became the first voyeur.
His punishment was swift and grim,
And there'll be no more peeps from *him*!

The Earl said: 'Wife! A deal's a deal —
Those savage taxes I'll repeal;
But just don't ask: 'Why aren't we rich?'
When we are *both* without a stitch!'

William the Conqueror

Duke William said: 'I'd like to see
Those English people ruled by me;
But since they cannot be persuaded,
They'll simply have to be invaded.

'Right now, the date I'm going to fix:
I'll do it in 1066.
Even the greatest ignoramus
Will know just why that year is famous.'

He told the Bayeux folk, when leaving:
'I need a tapestry — get weaving!
Please put my name on every panel.
And now, I'm off across the Channel.'

So William, in chain-mail apparelled,
Did furious battle with King Harold.
'There's one in the eye for *you*,' he said —
And poor King Harold dropped down dead.

The English cried: 'We can't resist 'em,
So let's adopt their feudal system.
A Baron gives you much less hassle
If you agree to be his vassal.'

They crowned King William in the Abbey,
And though some Saxons thought it shabby,
And found the change was quite a wrench,
Soon all the Court spoke Norman French.

You don't believe all this? Then look
Into King William's Domesday Book.

Saint George and the Dragon

A damsel cried: 'Help! Help, I pray —
A Dragon's dragging me away!'
'He'll soon,' said George, 'be dead and gone —
Just let me put my armour on.'

In forty minutes, he was dressed
And ready for the valiant quest.
He strode towards the Dragon's lair
And called: 'Come out! I know you're there!'
And sure enough, at once there came
From deep within, a gust of flame.

The Dragon growled: 'You'll never win her:
I'm going to have her for my dinner.
My fiery breath can make this cave
As good as any micro-wave!'

The cunning Saint replied: 'At least,
Have some hors d'oeuvres before the feast.'
And then, he started to advance,
A cocktail sausage on his lance.

The Dragon, always keen to gorge,
Came out and snarled: 'Well, thank you, George!'
His drooling jaws were open wide —
'GOTCHA!' our saintly hero cried,
And down his throat he thrust the lance —
The Dragon hadn't got a chance.

He gasped and gurgled and gyrated —
But soon he lay, decapitated.
The damsel said: 'God bless you, Sire —
I'll do whatever you desire.'

She winked — but George said: 'I'm a Saint,
And though I'd like to, ma'am, I mayn't.
The rules are strict when you are sainted;
Now, I must get my picture painted!'

And it was just as well he did,
For George's reputation slid:
The Vatican has even voted
That poor Saint George should be demoted.

If he had known he'd lose his crown,
He'd not have turned that damsel down.

Robin Hood

Robin believed that he was bigger
Than any legendary figure —
And so he'd growl, with irritation:
'Red Riding Hood is no relation!'

In BabyHood, he shot at sparrows
With teeny weeny bows and arrows.
No wonder that he grew to be
A champion at archery.

He cried: 'My fame I must assure —
I'll rob the rich, and help the poor.'
At which the Sheriff frowned and said:
'The fellow's nothing but a Red!
Henceforth, an outlaw he shall be.'
But Robin Hood said: 'That suits *me* —
If merry Robin thou abhorrest,
I'll go and live in Sherwood Forest.'

His followers were not too keen
To go and dress themselves in green,
And live on deer and home-made sherry
And keep pretending to be merry.
But Robin said: 'Laugh, Merry Men!
And now, I'll tell that joke again . . .'

Soon Friar Tuck and Little John
Began to wish they hadn't gone,
Young Will turned Scarlet, and the fun
Was too Much for the Miller's son.

The Merry Men went into action
To find their leader some distraction.
They brought Maid Marian, and Sherwood
At once became a His and Her Wood;
And while she listened to his quips
A smile was always on her lips.

What saintly patience men can find
In ladies of the Marian kind!

King John

King John appeared, in 1215,
At Runnymede, upon the Green.
He'd got the Barons' invitation
To join them for a celebration.

At first he'd cried: 'You must be barmy!'
But then he saw the Barons' army;
Since it was several thousand strong,
John said: 'Perhaps I'll come along.'

They told him: 'You'll become a martyr,
Unless you sign this Magna Charter!'
And then they started to unroll
A sixty-three-foot parchment scroll.

It curled right round the chair he sat in;
John grumbled: 'This is all in Latin!
But though it's hard to make it out,
I know just what it's all about:
More liberties you want to see
Given to *you*, instead of *me*!'

They said: 'You understand it fine —
So sign here, on the dotted line.'
But when the ink was hardly dry,
John thought: 'Those Barons I'll defy:
A foreign army I shall bring
To take back power for the King.'

But as his army crossed the Wash,
A great big wave came up, and — SPLOSH! —
It swept away his arms, and money.
The soldiers didn't think it funny:
They all of them went home to dry,
And didn't even say Goodbye.

King John, who couldn't take a beating,
Then killed himself, by over-eating:
Of lampreys (they're a kind of limpet)
He ate a feast, and didn't skimp it.

The greedy King was dead and gone —
So gourmets all, be warned by John:
If for Longevity your wish is,
Go easy on the sea-food dishes!

34

Richard the Third

The Duke of Gloucester yearned to be
Proclaimed King Richard, Number Three,
So those between him and the throne
He just rubbed out, like Al Capone.

His older brother, George, was found
Inside a butt of malmsey, drowned.
They say he sighed, as he was killed:
'It really tastes much nicer, chilled!'

Then Richard looked, with glances sour,
Upon the Princes in the Tower.
He growled: 'Kids make my blue blood boil,
Particularly when they're royal.
Though these are both my kith and kin,
I've simply got to do them in.'

Once he was King, his urgent mission
Was stamping out all opposition;
And even some who once were friends
Were meeting very sticky ends.

Soon, nobles said: 'He's had his fling —
It's time we had a different King.
Let's put an end to Richard's reign,
Before we all go down the drain.'

On Bosworth Field they tackled him;
King Richard said: 'The outlook's grim.
Though I don't plan to quit, of course,
I'd give my kingdom for a horse!'

A soldier said: 'My tip, your Grace,
Is Red Rose, in the second race.
In any case, I'll take a bet
That you're the last Plantagenet!'
And he was right: with Richard gone,
The House of Tudor carried on.

Our view of Richard Three today
Is largely based on Shakespeare's play:
Could Shakespeare's wicked King have been
Written to please his Tudor Queen?

William Caxton

William Caxton's eyes were glinting,
The glorious day he started printing.
The prospect might have pleased him less,
If he'd foreseen the Tabloid Press.

King Henry the Eighth

The eighth King Henry wined and dined,
And said: 'I'm not the Marrying Kind!'
He then proceeded, as you know,
To marry six wives in a row.

Which shows that Kings, however strong,
Can sometimes be completely wrong.
What's more, King Henry was inclined
Each time he wed, to change his mind.

Queen Catherine, his Number One,
Had come from Spain, that land of sun.
Each day she'd pick a bull to fight,
Then play the castanets all night.

The King said: 'I prefer the flute:
You get the Order of the Boot!'
But when he wrote and asked the Pope,
He got the answer: 'Not a hope!
A marriage is for keeps, of course —
Our Church does not permit Divorce.'

Said Henry: 'Since you take that tone,
I'll start a new Church of my own!'

There were six Queens in Henry's reign:
Two Annes, three Catherines, and a Jane;
And people said, as each went past,
'I always said it wouldn't last!'

Fair Anne Boleyn, his second Queen,
Quite lost her head, on Tower Green.
Jane Seymour died; then Anne of Cleeves
Was cast away, like autumn leaves.

Then Henry married Catherine Howard,
But she was faithless — Henry glowered;
He thundered: 'This has got to stop:
Madam, you're going for the chop!'
The last Queen stayed — did he adore her?
Or did he simply die before her?

For ages, Henry's record stood;
He'd get it back now, if he could!
Today, he'd emigrate for good,
And be the King of Hollywood.

Sir Francis Drake

Now when it came to taking chances,
No-one was bolder than Sir Francis.
All treasure-ships he liked to fire at —
In fact, the fellow was a pirate!

But Queen Elizabeth didn't mind;
Right there, aboard the Golden Hind,
She said to Drake: 'We're quite delighted —
So just kneel down, and you'll be knighted!'

When Spanish ships arrived in shoals
Drake finished off his game of bowls,
Then finished off the Spaniards too —
Which made King Philip very blue.

In Plymouth, statues of great size
Were raised to Drake; it's no surprise,
Considering what Sir Francis did,
They didn't raise one, in Madrid.

Sir Walter Raleigh

Though Queen Elizabeth fancied Walter,
She couldn't lead him to the altar,
For such a thing would not have been
Quite seemly in a Virgin Queen.

One day the Queen stepped out, and found
Sir Walter's cloak upon the ground.
She said, while treading on the vesture:
'I thank you, for that showy gesture!'
Then, to create a further stir,
He named Virginia after her.

When he returned, he brought the Queen
Her first royal drag of nicotine.
She breathed it in, then with surprise
She gaped, and gasped, and rolled her eyes.
When Raleigh said: 'Now ain't that swell?'
She spluttered: 'It will never sell!'

Sir Walter answered: 'Time will tell —
Meanwhile, I've something else as well:
Just wait until those royal lips
Have tasted my potato chips!'

The Queen said: 'If you've such bravado,
Go off and look for El Dorado!'

He searched, but nothing could he find;
His fortunes after that declined,
And when King James had come to power
He shut Sir Walter in the Tower.

Released, and then locked up again,
He sighed for Queen Elizabeth's reign:
Better to serve a Virgin Queen,
Than lose your head on Tower Green.
If she'd accepted when he wooed her,
There'd still have been a House of Tudor.

William Shakespeare

One day, rehearsing at the Globe,
Burbage said: 'Will, put on this robe.
I know the part that suits you most —
You're cast as Hamlet's Father's Ghost.'

His words made William Shakespeare wince —
He'd rather fancied playing the Prince.

But Burbage cried: 'It's got to be!'
Will said: 'To be or not to be,
That is the question now, of course.
I'd give my kingdom for a horse,
But when the hurly-burly's done
I'll fear no more the heat o' the sun,
Nor the furious winter's rage —
For truly, all the world's a stage.

'Get thee to a nunnery, I beseech,
And I'll once more unto the breach;
For truly, I know how to curse —
I won't put money in thy purse.
Though parting may be such sweet sorrow,
I'll leave tomorrow — and tomorrow!'

Said Burbage: 'Will, you try my patience —
You're always talking in quotations!
And I know very well you've taken
Each one of them from Francis Bacon.'

Then Shakespeare paled and said: 'Oh hell!
Burbage, I beg you not to tell.
I'll play the Ghost's part — yes, of course.
I'll even play King Richard's horse!'

Thus William Shakespeare's fame advances,
And few have ever heard of Francis.

Anne Hathaway

The day that Anne came on the scene,
Will Shakespeare was a mere eighteen.
At once, they fell in love and wed,
And at a banquet, William said:
'Anne Hath A Way my heart to thrill,
And now she also hath a Will.'

His speech did instantly delight her;
She cried: 'You ought to be a writer!'
Her eager words she'd soon regret:
He went and joined the Theatre Set.

Stuck there in Stratford, how Anne pined —
No husband, and three kids to mind.
The Shakespeares soon became gentility,
Yet something pained Anne's sensibility.
For many years she brooded on it:
Why didn't Will write *her* a Sonnet?'

Nell Gwynn

Nell Gwynn was fifteen years of age
When first she graced the English stage.
Her female charms quite won the day,
In parts boy-actors used to play.

A great career in acting beckoned —
But so did good King Charles the Second.
He said: 'Come, Nell, and keep me warm —
I like the way that you perform.'

Nell thought, as she was swiftly led
From royal box to royal bed:
'Well, even if I loathed the feller,
It sure beats being an orange-seller!'

Samuel Pepys

His wife remarked to Samuel Pepys:
'Your Diary's giving me the creeps.
What are you writing in that book?
Of course, I'd never take a look —
Besides, it's all in code, I fear.'
Said Pepys: 'How do you know, my dear?'

Sir Isaac Newton

An apple fell on Newton's cat,
And knocked the poor old creature flat.

His wife, who dearly loved a chat,
Said: 'What could be the cause of that?
I see it must be due, of course,
To some mysterious, downward Force,
That gives the fruit a sort of pull . . .'
Said Newton: 'Go and wind your wool!
Your mind is but an empty cavity
Unfit for matters of such Gravity.'

The cat groaned, as it lay there sprawled:
'I don't care *what* the Force is called!'
Newton cried: 'GRAVITY! I've said it!' —
And promptly went and took the credit.

50

George Frederick Handel

The Eighteenth-century musicians
Wrote most majestic compositions,
But none of them could hold a candle
To that flamboyant Mister Handel.

Though German-born, young Handel came
To England's court to make his name.
There, in the King's esteem he grew —
But then, the King was German too.

He dashed off operas by the score,
And oratorios galore.
(The latter were the most prestigious
Because their themes were so religious).

Though middle-brows may well admire works
Like *Music for the Royal Fireworks*,
Or say the *Water Music Suite*
Has got a most delightful beat,
The high-brows claim to have a ball
Listening to *Samson* or to *Saul*.

But Handel's great *Messiah* score
Has got a lot to answer for.
Each year, our local choirs implore us
To hear their *Hallelujah Chorus*,
And raucously their voices raise
To tell us *Sheep May Safely Graze*.

Oh, for a Christmas-time embargo
On everything but Handel's *Largo*!

Flora Macdonald and Bonnie Prince Charlie

After the Battle of Culloden,
Prince Charlie was subdued and sodden.
With mud-caked kilt and blood-stained brow
He moaned: 'I'm not so Bonnie now!'

Flora Macdonald told him: 'Prince —
Stay here, and you'll be mashed to mince.
I've got a boat — it's only wee,
But big enough for you and me.'

'Thank you,' said Charlie, 'let's be going —
And Flora, you can do the rowing.'
Then Flora, with her princely load,
Sang the Skye Boat Song as she rowed.

The Prince said: 'Skye's the place to halt —
They make a tasty Single Malt.
I'll gather herbs and heathers there
And mix them with that whisky rare,
And when the brew tastes good and gooey,
I'm going to call the stuff Drambuie!'

So gallant Flora saved the day,
And Bonnie Charlie got away.
He won no kingdom, that's for sure,
But boy, he left a great liqueur!

Doctor Johnson

Sam Johnson said to Boswell: 'Sir —
As a prodigious raconteur,
My life would be much more rewarding
If they'd invented tape-recording.

'Now, I've no wish to be censorious,
But this way, talk becomes laborious:
You faithfully record the Master —
But can't you write a little faster?'

Captain Cook

'The world is wide,' said Captain Cook,
'I think I'll go and take a look.'
So off he sailed, to the Pacific;
He thought the view was just terrific —
Nothing but sea to feast your eyes on,
Meeting the sky at each horizon.

He found it restful, but the crew
All wanted something else to do,
Like lying around on tropic isles
Where many a dusky maiden smiles,
And striking up a few romances
Between the hula-hula dances.

So Cook put on his full regalia
And said: 'I'll colonize Australia.'
But there, among the kangaroos,
A scouting party brought him news:
'The Aborigines, it appears,
Have been here forty thousand years.'

'I don't count *them*,' Cook answered back.
'They're naked — and besides, they're black.
I'm sure they wonder where we're from.'
He heard them mutter: 'Bloody Pom!'

Cook simply smiled and called: 'Goodby-ee!
I must dash off and find Hawaii.'
But those Hawaiians didn't like him —
He knew, when they began to strike him.

This last discovery he'd made:
Exploring is a dangerous trade.
So sail away, but understand —
It's really safer not to land.

Captain Bligh

Did Captain Bligh deserve the Mutiny?
The facts deserve a lot more scrutiny —
For Christian, his rebellious Mate,
Was full of most un-Christian hate.

He said: 'Come lads, let's all get mutinous —
We'll claim Bligh really put the boot in us!
We'll cast him off like so much dross,
Then Fletcher Christian will be boss.'

Bligh and his friends were set afloat
With no maps, in an open boat,
And Christian shouted with delight:
'Goodbye — and don't forget to write!'
Those rebel sailors little thought
He'd live to write a full report.

But Bligh's performance was terrific:
He could have starred in *South Pacific*.
For seven weeks he sailed that ocean —
His landing made a great commotion.
The islanders, in quite a state,
Said: 'Boy, that guy can navigate!'

No wonder Bligh had caused a rumpus:
He'd done it all without a compass.

But Fletcher Christian, foolish chap,
Just found a dot upon the map,
And all his men moaned: 'We're in bits —
This Pitcairn Island is the pits!'

And Christian thought, 'Next time I try
To tangle with a bloke like Bligh,
I'll get my man, like any Mountie,
Before I go and take the *Bounty*!'

Madame Tussaud

Madame Tussaud said: 'France will be
Too revolutionary for *me*!'
But England now will be a doddle
For someone who can make a model.'

The English found her name a tease —
It sounded very like a sneeze;
But soon they all were making tracks
To see her famous House of Wax.

Now, tourists flock to see the show,
And cry: 'That's just like So-and-So!'
Though sometimes, when they prod and feel,
They're shocked to find the person's real!

It is the greatest accolade
To have your waxwork figure made.
But fame is fickle, fame is short,
And so it's kind to spare a thought
For those who, once of great renown,
Are taken off, and melted down. . .

63

Lord Nelson

At twelve, Horatio went to sea —
Though that was young, we must agree,
He soon grew up, and set his heart
On bashing General Bonaparte.

He lost an eye, and then an arm,
But clearly didn't lose his charm,
For when he courted Lady Emma
These minor faults caused no dilemma.
One day she told him, with a sigh:
'England expects . . . and so do I!'

'Why aren't you home?' asked Lady Nelson;
Horatio said: 'I've something else on —
So splice the mainbrace, tie the lanyards —
I'm going off to fight the Spaniards.'

He fought some furious campaigns
Against the Spaniards, French, and Danes.
When through his telescope he'd stare
And cry: 'Good Lord! There's nothing there!'
Lieutenant Hardy would reply:
'Why don't you try the other eye?'
But though he was right-eye-and-armless,
Napoleon found him far from harmless.

When brave Lord Nelson met his death,
He whispered, with his final breath:
'Come, kiss me Hardy now, and tell
Emma I sent a kiss as well.
How gladly I enjoyed her beauty —
But still, thank God, I've done my duty,
And though my morals stand at zero,
They'll still be calling me a hero!'

And there he stands, sedate and solemn,
Among the pigeons, on his Column.

J.M.W. Turner

The painter, J. M. W. Turner,
Said: 'I've a lovely little earner:
My canvasses I'll splash and splosh
Until they're utterly awash.'

'As people gaze at them, agog,
I'll say they're called *Rain*, *Steam*, or *Fog*.
The experts then will murmur: "Golly!"
And give me loads and loads of lolly.'

Some critics cried: 'The man's insane —
Who wants to look at fog and rain?'
But Turner quipped: 'If I, by chance,
Had been born later, and in France,
And painted sun instead of mist,
I'd be a French Impressionist.
So shut your mouths, and know your places,
Or you'll have egg upon your faces.'

Turner was right to say: 'I'm great!' —
His work's now featured at the Tate.

Queen Victoria

The day the fourth King William died,
'Long live the Queen!' the people cried.
The Queen replied: 'I will, my dears!' —
And lived for more than eighty years.

Though she has often been accused
Of not being easily amused,
The laughs were surely very few
When Gladstone was haranguing you.

One nineteenth-century historian
Remarked: 'Her views are quite Victorian,
And yet, not *every* joy she shuns:
She's had five daughters, and four sons!'

Her husband Albert was her idol;
Without him, she was suicidal.
So that his fame would not grow dim,
Victoria named things after him.

Years later, we can all still see 'em:
Albert's Embankment, and Museum,
His Bridge, Memorial, and Hall,
Where Promenaders have a ball.

Victoria reigned on and on,
Until the century was gone.
Meanwhile her son, Prince Albert Edward,
Grew fond of taking ladies bed-ward.

He led a life of lust and levity,
And blamed it on his Mum's longevity:
He must do *something* while he waited
Until the throne had been vacated.

Today, the Heir prefers to lecture
On inner city architecture.

The Brontë Sisters

Charlotte, Emily and Anne
Sighed: 'We must do the best we can,
Although life's far from jovial here:
The Yorkshire Moors are damp and drear,
Our Dad's as mad as old King Lear —
And Brother Branwell's on the beer!
But we'll defy the mournful mists
By all becoming novelists.'

So Emily researched at nights
The atmosphere for *Wuthering Heights*.
Her sisters wondered, was it true
She was researching Heathcliff too?
Charlotte's *Jane Eyre* was grim, but groovy,
And Orson Welles was in the movie.

They knew their writings might not strike
A publisher as lady-like,
And so, to pander to the prim,
They each took on a pseudonym.
They were three brothers, surnamed Bell,
And found their books did rather well.

They travelled little — no Miss Brontë
Was ever seen at Cannes or Monte;
In fact, they rarely ventured forth
From that stone village in the north.
But Yorkshire folk would all declare:
'Our county's best — why go elsewhere?'

Yet if the sisters felt confined
They never seemed to speak their mind.
(Which marks them out from Chekhov's Three,
Who yearned for Moscow constantly
And never ceased to whinge and whine —
And never wrote a single line!)

But these three daughters of a vicar
Have lit a flame that will not flicker.
Some people thought them a bizarre lot,
Yet Anne, and Emily, and Charlotte
Wrote books whose glory still endures
Up there upon the Yorkshire Moors.

Charles Dickens

When Dickens's long career began,
He wrote on the instalment plan;
Each month his readers scanned the capers
Of Mister Pickwick, in the Papers.

His novels touched them to the core —
Like Oliver, they asked for more;
And thanks to Ebenezer Scrooge,
His fame and fortune both grew huge.

Dickens was happy to perform —
His readings took the world by storm.
The public flocked to hear and see;
They loved his voice — and so did he.
Americans all thought him swell —
His waistcoats dazzled them, as well.

We must be glad he took the stage
Before the television age,
For very soon he'd learn the ropes
And earn big money, writing soaps;
And doubtless, now, his watching ghost
Just yearns to be a chat-show host.

Florence Nightingale

When Florence said she'd just adore
To go to the Crimean War,
Her parents, shaken to the core,
Demanded: 'Flo! Whatever for?'

But off she went, to be a nurse;
The Generals thought she was a curse —
Why must the woman make a scene
If bandages were not quite clean?

There were decisions to be made
Like ordering the Light Brigade:
'Charge, chaps! Although the guns are menacin',
You'll be immortalized by Tennyson!'

The privates, though, in every camp
Just loved *The Lady with the Lamp*.
Now nurses, thanks to her obsession,
Are in a highly praised profession —
But still, like Florence's brigade,
They're overworked, and underpaid.

Doctor Livingstone

When Livingstone, a Scot by birth,
Decided to explore the earth,
He said: 'I'd like to make my mark
Upon a Continent that's Dark.'
So off to Africa he went
With just a Bible and a tent.

Soon he declared, with great euphoria:
'Look! I've discovered Lake Victoria!
And there's Victoria Falls as well —
Oh, what a tale I'll have to tell!'

The folk who'd lived upon that shore
For several hundred years or more
Refrained from saying: 'David — steady!
We have discovered them already;
And, though we're sure it seems a shame,
We've given them a different name.'

Instead, they said: 'Doc, you're the Boss:
We'll show you rivers you can cross,
And far-flung mountains, crowned with frost.'
(They knew he'd get completely lost!)

As David wandered round and round,
One day there came a curious sound —
He heard the voice of Stanley boom:
'You're Doctor Livingstone, I presume?'
The Doctor, thinking him a bore,
Said: 'No, you want the house next door!'

But Stanley knew a thing or two;
He cried: 'Come, Dave, I know it's you —
And now I shall be famous too!'

The moral is, if *you* want fame,
Seek someone with a famous name
Lost in a Continent that's Dark,
And make a fatuous remark!

Charles Darwin

Charles Darwin, when he got the chance,
Sailed round the world, collecting plants;
Then he retired into his study —
Some thought he was a fuddy-duddy,
But what a storm the man unleashes
Writing *The Origin of Species*!

83

Charles Darwin smiles to see them fret,
And says: 'You ain't seen nothin' yet!
If that's a book you'd like to ban,
Try reading *The Descent of Man*!'

Victorians in High Society
Complained: 'This man lacks all propriety —
Even our skivvies and our flunkies
Can't be descended from the monkeys!'

As for the bishops and the clerics,
He sent them all into hysterics:
For years they'd taught us to believe
We came from Adam and from Eve.

They thundered: 'Let this jackanapes
Go to the Planet of the Apes!
Whoever preaches Evolution
Will face a holy retribution.'

And still, some hold the firm opinion
The Devil lurks in things Darwinian;
But if they visit any zoo,
They might come round to Darwin's view.

Mrs Beeton

The guests who dined with Mrs Beeton
Were sure to find they'd overeaten.
Whole herds of cows and shoals of fishes
Were used to make her famous dishes.

She had a bucket as a scoop
To ladle out the oxtail soup.
The whipped cream piled upon her trifle
Rose higher than the Tower of Eiffel.

In every dish, her books inform us,
The quantities must be enormous;
For Mrs Beeton took the view:
Why use one egg, when twelve will do?

How those Victorian gents indulged!
No wonder that their waistcoats bulged.
They gorged on goose, munched mounds of
    mutton,
And then undid another button.

Oh, lucky gents! They'd think us bats
To fear cholesterol and fats.
They exercised, when they were able,
By simply lurching from the table.

Now, in this era of the Slimmer,
Poor Mrs Beeton's fame grows dimmer.
Though many still enjoy her diet,
They have to do it, on the quiet.

FIDOUGH

Henry Irving

Some actors found it quite unnerving
To take the stage with Henry Irving.
He'd choose his cast, and when they all
Came to the first rehearsal call,
He'd exercise his Thespian art
By reading every single part.

Off stage, his joy was making merry
With that great actress, Ellen Terry.
She was, though some might think it shady,
In every sense his Leading Lady.

Irving enjoyed a great career;
The people flocked to see and hear
When in the theatre he'd appear
As Hamlet, Romeo, or Lear.

Now, Theatre Knights are two a penny,
But Irving was the first of many.
They said: 'It's just what he deserves —
I hope he won't get First Knight nerves!'

Mrs Pankhurst

Of all campaigners in the nation
Who fought for women's liberation
The one we really ought to thank first
Is that great fighter, Mrs Pankhurst.

She and her daughters took the view
The vote was every woman's due;
With pride they raised their banners high,
And VOTES FOR WOMEN was their cry.
They suffered beatings-up and jailings,
And chained themselves to lots of railings.

Churchill, and many men of note,
Said women shouldn't have a vote,
And thought that men should rule the lives
Of everyone, including wives.

Those chauvinists — what did they fear?
No clubs? No pubs? A ban on beer?
Or was it something much more sinister —
A woman, chosen as Prime Minister?

Lord Baden-Powell

Lord Baden-Powell gained great prestige
Defending Mafeking from siege —
A feat which was, though hardly fun,
A great Relief for everyone.

'The Boer War taught me,' he declared,
'That chaps should learn to Be Prepared;
Tie knots, light fires, and put up tents,
And generally behave like gents.
And to encourage such improvement,
I'm going to found the Boy Scout Movement.'

He said a Scout is brave and kind,
And clean in body and in mind,
Makes sure his tent is never damp,
And nothing but the fire is camp.

If lustful thoughts his mind should sour,
He simply goes and takes a shower —
First making sure, as he's been told,
The water's very, very cold.

In spite of such austere regimes
World-wide success has crowned his dreams,
And villagers as well as townies
Are Scouts and Guides, and Cubs and Brownies.

B. P.'s great fame will never dim —
They named a petrol after him!
There's just one thing I puzzle at:
Why did he wear that silly hat?

W. G. Grace

Grace felt it really wasn't Cricket,
Expecting him to leave the wicket.
'Howzat?!' they cried; Grace heard the shout,
And instantly replied: 'Not out!'

One Umpire said: 'I hate to trouble you,
But Doctor Grace, you're LBW.'
The great man answered: 'Not at all —
You really should have called No Ball!'

And even when the bails went flying,
And on the ground the stumps were lying,
He'd simply pick them up and say:
'There's quite a heavy wind today!'

In Grace's last great game, they say
He stayed out batting there all day,
The next day, and the next day too;
His bushy beard just grew and grew,
Till Grace, playing forward with his bat,
Tripped on his beard and fell down flat.

The fielders gazed, amazed to see
The large, unconscious W. G.,
And as they crowded round about
The Umpire smiled and said: 'He's out!'

Rolls and Royce

Said Rolls to Royce: 'We'll both go far
If we design a motor-car;
A car so very, very posh
That everyone will murmur: "Gosh!"
And peer at it, amazed and curious,
To see a motor so luxurious.'

Their first machine had so much power,
It went at thirty miles an hour.
As down the road they were proceeding,
The pair of them were booked for speeding.

Said Royce to Rolls: 'We've made a stir.
I love to hear that engine purr!
We've every reason to be proud —
But is the clock a trifle loud?'

John Logie Baird

When first of all, John Logie Baird
Transmitted pictures, people stared.
They said: 'What *does* he think he's doing?'
If Baird could see the stuff *we're* viewing,
He might be turning his attention
Towards some other new invention.

Agatha Christie

When people read a Christie thriller,
They find it hard to spot the killer.
But, when Agatha'd begun it,
Did she herself know just Whodunnit?

Or did she, as each corpse fell dead,
Frown anxiously and scratch her head,
Lay down her pen, and say: 'Tomorrow,
I'll have to call in Hercule Poirot.'?